THE PRIDE

OF

YORKSHIRE

by

Ron and Marlene Freethy

© Frank Morley Books

Published December 1992
by Frank Morley Books
Unit 2, Racecommon Road
Barnsley, West Yorkshire

ISBN 0 9520652 0 7

Warehouse & Orders
Telephone: 0836 781571
Unit 2, Racecommon Road
Barnsley, West Yorkshire

Printed & Bound by:
Manchester Free Press,
Paragon Mill, Jersey Street,
Manchester, M4 6FP
Tel: 061–236 8822
Fax: 061–236 9980

INTRODUCTION

Yorkshire has always been known as the Proud County but even it's hardest critics admit that the county has a lot to be proud of. So much, in fact, that the choice of what to leave out was a very hard one.

This book has taken a long hard look at England's largest county and has captured in clear photographs all that visitors, tourists and the people of Yorkshire themselves should look up to and look for when in God's Own Country. Ron and Marlene Freethy who compiled the book are no strangers to the county having written six other books on the area. Ron is well known to TV watchers as a nature expert and walking guide, while Marlene has always accompanied him and added copy to his wonderful photographs.

This is a book to enjoy, to savour, either to remember visits or to look forward to bringing these pictures to life. It can even be useful as a guide, giving you somewhere to head for on outings to the county. Whatever reason you are now holding the book may we wish you enjoyment as you sample . . .

THE PRIDE OF YORKSHIRE.

Ron Freethy

About the Authors

Ron Freethy is President of the North East Lancashire Rambler's Association and has made many television and radio programmes. With his wife Marlene he has written several walking books and volumes on tourism throughout the country.

Marlene Freethy with Bono ... always an excuse for a walk

Also by Frank Morley Books . . .

Postcards of South Yorkshire

BARNSLEY • DONCASTER • ROTHERHAM • SHEFFIELD

A nostalgic look at the towns & cities of South Yorkshire through postcards of the past.

Available now at £4·95
ISBN 0 9520652 1 5

Ilkley is lucky to have its town museum housed in a magnificent Elizabethan Manor House just below the church.

The old packhorse bridge over the River Wharfe at Ilkley is one of the finest in Yorkshire. It is in excellent repair but these days is only used by pedestrians.

Everyone has heard the song 'On Ilkley Moor Bahr Tat', but in summer nobody wears a hat as they enjoy a picnic below the rock formation which dominates the moor.

1. Otley was the birthplace of Thomas Chippendale whose fame spread from Yorkshire throughout the world. A plaque commemorates his birth in 1718.

2. The plaque on the old Manor House celebrating the birth of Chippendale in 1718.

The White Cottage at Harrogate was once the paybox leading to one of the springs of water for which the town has long been famous.

The Royal Baths at Harrogate. To the left of the crossing a lady stands ready to sample the free water which still issues from the spring.

This structure is called Tuit's Well, one of Harrogate's many famous mineral springs. It stands high above the town on what was once an open moor. The local name for the lapwing is the tuit.

1. The River Nidd flows beneath the magnificent railway viaduct at Knaresborough.

2. The market cross at Knaresborough. Among the buildings to the right of the cross is a chemist's shop said to be the oldest in the world.

1. Many buildings still stand among the ruins of Knaresborough Castle including the old court house seen here across a lawn full of the colourful flowers of crocus.

2. Although it is rather plain looking on the outside Knaresborough's church of St. John the Baptist has some magnificent monuments inside its lofty interior.

3. The Slingsby Chapel inside Knaresborough church. It was one of this family who in 1571 discovered the Tuit Well at Harrogate which was then only a hamlet on his estate.

The Watermill has been recently restored and is one of the finest Inns in Nidderdale. It is situated just beyond Pateley Bridge.

How Stean Gorge is one of the beauty spots of Nidderdale and from the cafe a number of well marked paths lead through ancient rock formations and river scenery.

1. *This wonderful stalactite has been forming for thousands of years beneath the Yorkshire Dales at Stump Cross.*

2. *Looking like a huge Cathedral with its organ, this formation is one of the many wonders of the Stump Cross Caverns.*

1. The view down Nidderdale from Middlemoor churchyard reminds some of the Lake District and others of Switzerland. To us it is just glorious Yorkshire!

2. Middlemoor church is perched on a hill at the head of Nidderdale.

Brimham Rocks near Pateley Bridge, look like the remnants of some ancient civilisation but have been caused by centuries of weathering of the sandstone rocks. The area is owned by the National Trust who have set up a car park and Information Centre.

The Bridge at Richmond crossing the River Swale has been a favourite of artists for many years and is a delight to see whatever the time of the year

Richmond Castle viewed from an ancient green below the town. The sheer strength of this bastion enabled its owners to dominate large areas of Upper Swaledale.

Just downstream of Richmond close to the banks of the Swale are the haunting ruins of Easby, a 12th century Cistercian monastery. It is connected to Richmond via a delightful riverside path.

1   The history of Swaledale, especially its industry of lead mining, is graphically explained in a folk museum in the busy village of Reeth.

2   The Tan Hill Inn stands at the head of Swaledale directly on the Pennine Way and from which there are splendid views into Durham. It has become so popular with walkers that an extension was built during 1992. There is always a welcoming fire at the Tan Hill and the bar snacks cater for good appetites

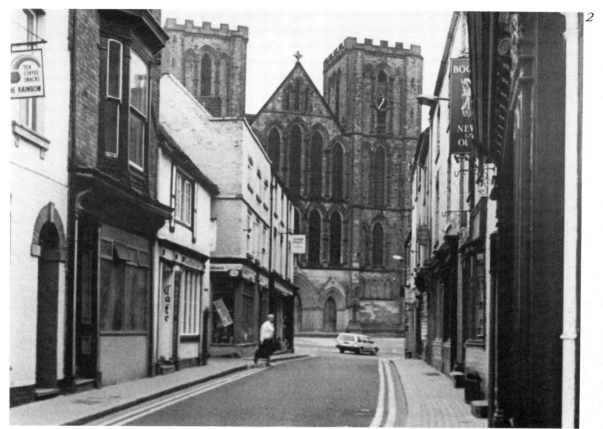

1. The old Wakeman's House at Ripon is now the Tourist Information Centre facing the square. A reminder of the old days is enacted each evening when the curfew is sounded from the square.

2. Ripon Cathedral soaring above the narrow streets of the town is a very real rival to York Minster.

1

1. Fountain's Abbey near Ripon is one of the finest remaining Cistercian Abbeys in Europe. Constant work is needed to maintain its wonderful fabric constructed between the 12th and 16th centuries.

2. This wonderfully vaulted room, a gem of Norman architecture, was only the cellar of Fountain's Abbey. It gives just a small clue to the magnificence of the rest of the monastery.

1

1 When Fountain's Abbey was dissolved in the 1530s much of its masonry went into the buildings of Fountain's Hall. In 1931 the Hall almost became the residence of the Duke and Duchess of York who later became George VI and Queen Elizabeth, the parents of the present Queen. Now open to the public, along with Fountain's Abbey this house is one of the most famous in Europe as an example of early 17th century architecture.

2 The church of St. Michael's and All Angels at Hubberholme is an ideal place to join a footpath following the River Wharfe towards its source.

3 Hubberholme's church is one of the few to have retained its rood loft following the Reformation in the mid 16th century. It also shows how church design at first differed very little from the construction of a barn.

1.

1. Halton Gill is one of a string of delightful hamlets set into the hills of Upper Wharfedale.

2. The sheer beauty of Halton Gill set into the limestone hills of Wharfedale is staggering.

The Falcon in Arncliffe shows how the first pubs evolved. Farmers brewed ale for their workers and sold the surplus to visitors. This Inn is still half farm and half pub with a wonderful atmosphere.

Arncliffe is a pretty village almost at the head of Littondale which is a side valley running off Wharfedale. The pump is still a feature of the green.

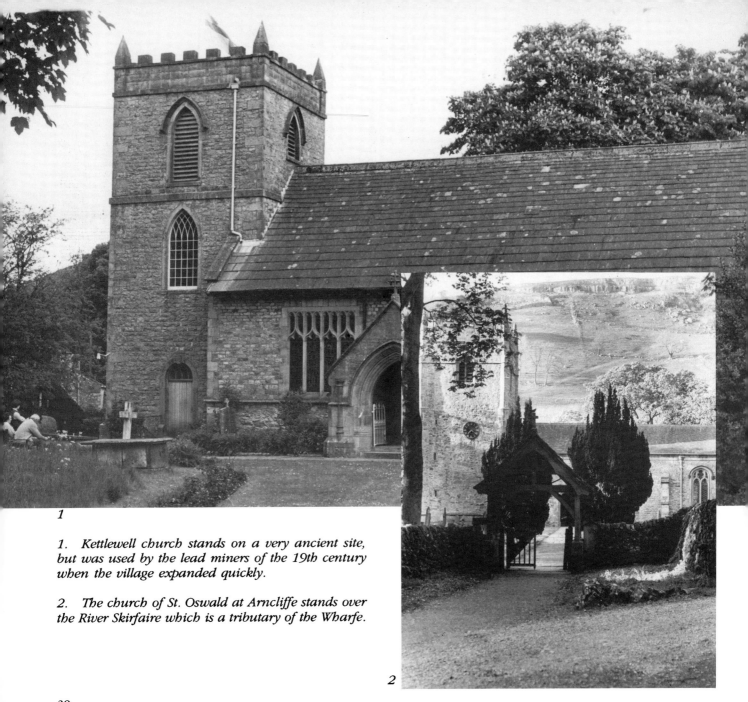

1. Kettlewell church stands on a very ancient site, but was used by the lead miners of the 19th century when the village expanded quickly.

2. The church of St. Oswald at Arncliffe stands over the River Skirfaire which is a tributary of the Wharfe.

Kettlewell, with its bridge over the Wharfe, is popular with walkers many of whom carry light tents with them on their treck through Wharfedale.

1. Kilnsey Cragg with its Visitors' Centre, ample parking and good fishing is one of Wharfedale's treasures. The Crag is also much used by rock climbers.

2. The limestone pavements above Grassington can be deserted even in summer and here grow some of Britain's rarest plants.

Morris Dancers performing at Grassington, a village which was right at the heart of the lead mining industry in Wharfedale.

Grassington has no parish church but nearby on the banks of the Wharfe is the hamlet of Linton. St. Michael and All Angels dates back to Saxon times and is one of the most beautiful churches in Yorkshire.

1. Linton Falls are beautiful rather than spectacular and were created to power the textile mills when industry was small and village based.

2. St. Wilfrid's church at Burnsall dates back to the 12th century and is seen here from the road. It can also be seen from the pretty footpath which leads along the River Wharfe from Linton to Burnsall.

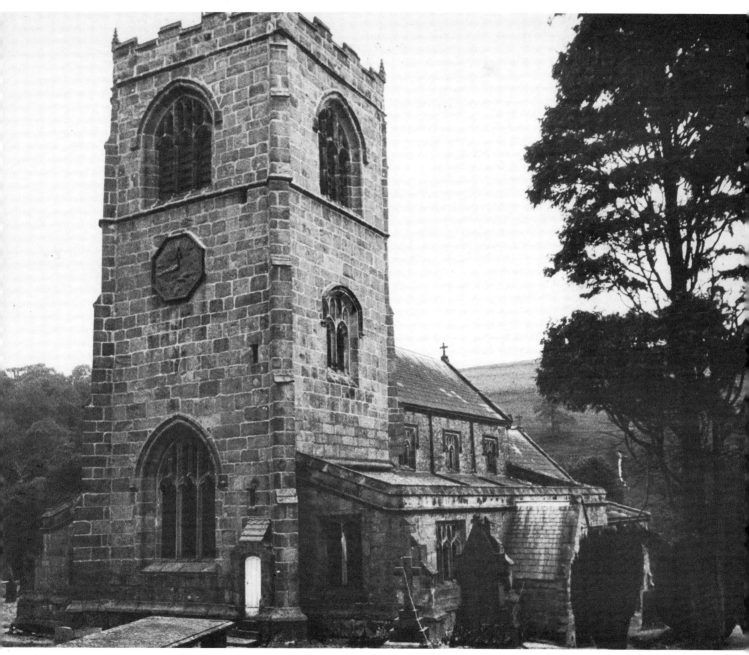

Burnsall Grammar School is still in use but is now used by junior children. It dates back to Elizabethan times when it had a reputation for learning recognised throughout Wharfedale.

A winter scene of Burnsall Bridge which is overlooked by attractive houses and hotels whilst the village green to the right of the bridge is a popular spot for summer picnics.

Barden Tower was one of the many castles which Lady Anne Clifford restored in the middle of the 17th century in defiance first of Cromwell and then of Charles II. The tower overlooks Barden Bridge between Burnsall and Bolton Abbey.

A brave couple cross the stepping stones over the River Wharfe at Bolton Abbey. The more sensible (or cowardly) photographer is standing on the wooden footbridge.

Beamsley Alms Houses in Wharfedale, near Bolton Abbey were commenced by Lady Anne Clifford's mother and completed by the grand old Lady herself around 1650. Her coat of arms still shows prominently over the entrance.

Although it is a little bit off the main road through Wensleydale, West Burton with its huge green is so attractive that it must be visited by all who love the Dales.

The River Ure crashes over Aysgarth falls and above stands the historic church of St. Andrew, one of the largest in Yorkshire and on a site dating back to Saxon times.

It is not always possible to enjoy wandering across the Ure at Aysgarth. After rain a torrent of peaty brown water crashes over the falls.

1. *Close to the Upper Falls at Aysgarth is the Yore Mill. It is now a museum of old carriages and tells the history of the turnpike roads. It once wove the red cloth from which the uniforms of Garibaldi's Italian army were made.*

2. *East Witton church dominates an estate village at the front and to its rear are the atmospheric and haunting ruins of Jervaulx Abbey.*

Jervaulx Hall was built during the 17th century using stone taken from the Cistercian Abbey nearby.

The ruins of Jervaulx Abbey are reached from a car park across a very pretty meadow. It is always open and payment for entry is by means of a small honesty box at the gate.

Jervaulx was built by the Cistercians in the 12th century and was dissolved by Henry VIII in the 1530s. Many of the splendid Norman arches remain.

Spennithorne stands at the confluence of the Ure and its tributary the Cover. In the churchyard stands one of the most unusual monuments in Yorkshire. It is a golden cross looted by the British Major General Straubenzee from Sebastapol barracks in 1854 during the Crimean War.

1. *York Minster is one of the world's great churches which thankfully has been restored following a potentially disastrous fire. All the effort and the money have been worth it.*

2. *The choir in York Minster is a majestic mix of light and colour highlighting some of the greatest wood carvings in Europe.*

3. *The Buttermarket and behind it the church of St. Giles are both reminders of Pontefract's role as an ancient market town.*

3

3

1. The ruins of Pontefract Castle are situated in the town park. The castle was the setting for Shakespeare's play Richard II.

2. Not far from the M1 near Wakefield is the Yorkshire Sculpture Park, one of the North of England's most exciting places. This is truly art in the open air with plenty of parking and cafes. It is open free of charge.

3. Tadcaster is one of Yorkshire's oldest towns dating back to Roman times. They appreciated the quality of its water and so do the modern brewers for the town is dominated by the two rivals Samuel and John Smith.

Tadcaster stands on the Wharfe and there are some beautiful riverside walks to explore slowly. On return strollers should remember that if they are thirsty some of the best beer in the world is brewed here.

Wetherby is a fine old market town. This picture shows the old shambles which is where the butchers killed and sold their meat. On market day it would really have been a shambles!

1. Almondbury Hill above Huddersfield was settled before written history began. The "castle", however, was built to celebrate Queen Victoria's Diamond Jubilee in 1897.

2. The view of industrial Huddersfield from Almondbury hill is beautiful especially since the clean air acts of the 1950s. The smoke from the chimneys of the woollen mills has been reduced partly because of the reduction in trade in recent years but also because industry is more conservation minded.

Almondbury once dominated Huddersfield, but is now a mere suburb of the industrial town. Opposite Almondbury church there are some of the oldest half-timbered buildings in Yorkshire.

There are not many of the old blue "Dr Who" police boxes left in the country, but there is a fine example on the main road through Almondbury.

1

1. Golcar is a fine example of an industrial village. This steep track leads down from the informative little museum. This tells the history of the woollen industry in the valleys of the Rivers Calder and Colne.

2. David Essex takes the first trip aboard the Marsden Shuttle on the Huddersfield Narrow Canal. The Information Centre is shown behind.

A horse drawn barge on its way from Hebden Bridge to Walkley's Clog Mill. Regular trips are run during the summer and even out of season by appointment.

1. Although it is still operational Hebden Bridge Station is still as interesting as a mid Victorian museum. Its wooden signs are still in a wonderful state of repair.

2. In the days when wool weaving was done by hand the "pieces" produced in cottages were brought to be sold at the Piece Hall at Halifax. Each room was the office of a wool merchant who bought and exported the pieces. Fortunately this lovely building, which became redundant as factories evolved, has been restored and adds a unique atmosphere to the market.

Wherever brass band music is mentioned Black Dyke Mills usually springs to mind. They are based at Queensbury near Bradford. Here is the Gothic style memorial erected to mourn the death of Prince Albert and which was unveiled in May 1863. It still dominates the cross roads at Queensbury.

Now a rest home, Prospect House on the main road through Queensbury was the home of John Foster, the founder of one of the most famous mills in the world.

1

1. Few people these days realise that Bradford was once famous for the manufacture of motor cars. These Jowetts are on display in Bradford's Industrial Museum which also has a number of vans as well as the famous Javelins.

2. This view from Bingley church shows how little the old town centre has altered since the 17th century despite the modern road which now slices its way through.

The five rise locks at Bingley on the Leeds to Liverpool are regarded as one of the engineering wonders of the Canal Age.

The Leeds to Liverpool canal is overlooked by Titus Salt's mill at Saltaire, the village he built for his workers. In the summer a water bus operates a service between Saltaire and Bingley.

1. The Congregational Church built at Saltaire by Sir Titus Salt has a distinctly Greco Roman feel about it.

2. The River Aire flows alongside the Leeds to Liverpool Canal at Saltaire. In the summertime rowing boats can be hired and snacks enjoyed in the open air. The scene has changed hardly at all since the 1870s.

1. *Just outside Skipton is Elslack. All Saints church is seldom visited because the village is now off the main route of all modern roads.*

2. *The grave of a most remarkable schoolmaster is found at Elslack. Enoch Hall was first a soldier under Wellington and was one of the men chosen to guard Napoleon after Waterloo on the island of St. Helena.*

3. *Several Turnpike roads run through Skipton. This old toll house has now been converted into an attactive residence.*

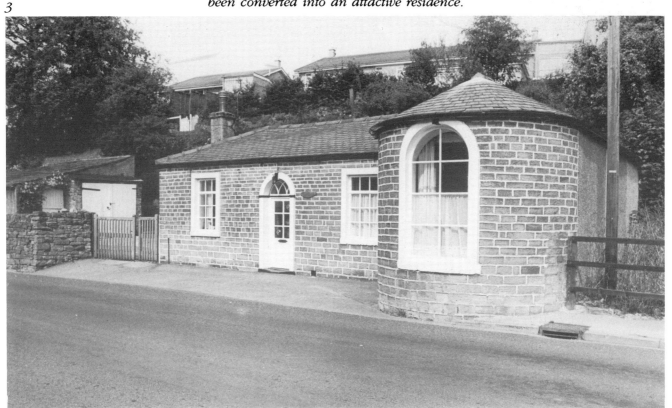

Now just a quiet hamlet Elslack lies on the site of a small Roman fort and thus was once much more important than nearby Skipton.

The Tempest Arms at Elslack is one of the oldest and most popular pubs in Yorkshire.

1

2

1. Embsay Steam Railway describes itself as the "Friendly Line" and has an ambition to provide a link between Skipton in Airedale with Bolton Abbey in Wharfedale.

2. Embsay Railway is seen at its best when the Santa Special operates. Here Thomas the Tank Engine is hard at work.

3. The Leeds to Liverpool Canal is always busy at Gargrave. Here the line of the canal follows the valley of the River Aire.

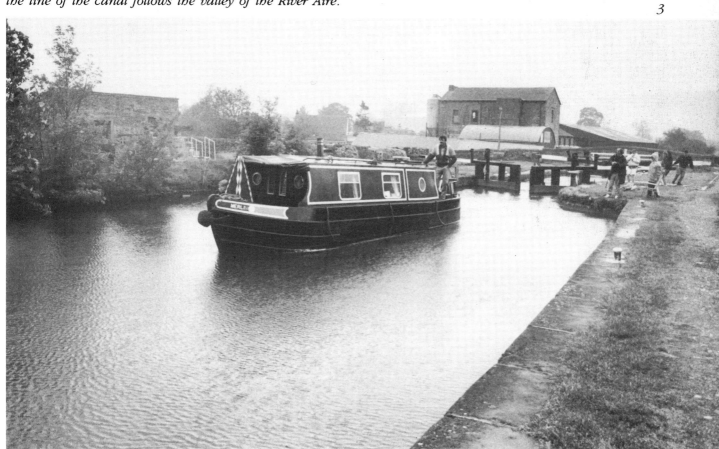

3

1. Because it is so close to Malham the little village of Airton with its stocks, squatter's house and village green, is often passed by visitors. This is a pity because it is one of Yorkshire's gems.

2. Malham village does not have a church. This is situated nearby at Kirkby Malham. To the right of the picture is one of the most unusual graves in Britain. A stream runs through it as a wife separated from her soldier husband for so long decided that if they were separated by water during life why not continue this in death?

2

This is Aire Springs between Malham and Kirkby Malham. This lonely and beautiful spot is said to be the source of the River Aire.

Whilst Malham Tarn and Cove plus Gordale Scar get all the publicity Janet's Fosse waterfall often takes a minor role. This is a pity for it is a lovely spot. Black Labradors love it too.

Scarborough has everything — a wonderful harbour, seaside entertainments and a magnificent castle dominating the headland.

During the 18th and 19th centuries Scarborough developed into one of the major Spa towns of Europe. Here at the Spa Pavilion there is still the feel of Victorian elegance about it.

Few castles have a more imposing entrance than Scarborough, now splendidly maintained by English Heritage.

1. *Anne Brontë on holiday from Haworth, died in Scarborough and is buried in the shadow of the castle.*

2. *Although Scarborough is a modern town it still has an enviable history. The House of Mystery museum was once the property of Richard III.*

Scarborough on a busy day providing entertainment for thousands of visitors. No resort has such a fine castle overlooking its shoreline. Scarborough has been the "Lung of Working Yorkshire" for more than a century.